A gift for:

From:

_____

Published by Hallmark Books,
a division of Hallmark Cards, Inc.,
Kansas City, MO 64141
Visit us on the Web at Hallmark.com.

Writers: Chris Conti, Bill Gray, and Dan Taylor
Editor: Megan Langford
Art Director: Kevin Swanson
Designer and Production Artist: Dan Horton

ISBN: 978-1-59530-246-5
BOK2101

Printed and bound in China

HUMOR FOR BOOMERS

Older and Wiser

(and Funnier!)

gift books

THEN

NOW

OK, so maybe you can trust some people over 30. And that "hope I die before I get old" thing? Too late for that. Tie-dye has turned to plaid. "Turn on" is something you only do to the TV. Your bathing suit covers more than your entire outfit used to. Jumpin' Jack Flash has gas, gas, gas.

And you still don't know what the hell a Gadda Da-Vida is.

Funny thing, though. On the way to becoming older than you ever thought you'd be, you've learned that middle age isn't so bad after all. Slowing down gives you more time to enjoy the scenery. We may not have been the Greatest Generation, but we were definitely the coolest.

So join us, won't you, as we go day trippin' down memory lane.

Things You Tell Yourself Are Just As Good As What They Replace

Decaf coffee

Diet soda

Titanium ball and socket joint

Three Most Commonly Forgotten Things

1. Keys

2. Reading glasses

3. What was the question?

Phrases You Thought You Would Never Use That Really ARE Handy

Not under my roof, you won't!

Where are my reading glasses?

It's a dry heat.

You kids go ahead without me.

Nurse!

Sure, video games are all well and good,
but do any of these kids nowadays know the thrill
of a whistling yo-yo?

Wait—the president is younger than us?
Is that even legal?

Boomers don't need anything more than
a young person needs: frequent naps, soft food,
and close proximity to a bathroom.

If you're lucky, not every single thing you ever
made fun of old people for will happen to you.
Most of us aren't that lucky.

Hazing rituals for people your age.

Whatever doesn't kill you
(or hurt your knees,
back, shoulders, or feelings)
makes you stronger.

Musical Arguments That Cannot Be Won

Cutest Beatle?

Meaning of "Stairway" played backward?

Who's so vain?

Did the Monkees really play their instruments?

The actual lyrics to "Louie, Louie"?

Boomer Tip #17

Squinting isn't sexy. Tough, maybe.

Intimidating, possibly. But not sexy.

Also, it's not tough or intimidating

if you're in a restaurant

and can't make out the entrées.

Good Things About Being the Oldest Person at Work

You don't have to help anyone move.
(Because no one even asks you.)

You can finish the birthday cake.
Nobody's gonna say nothin'.

You don't have to worry if orthodontics
are covered by your insurance.
(Orthopedics, though, are another story.)

You can probably special-order a really nice chair.

Places Where It's Always OK to Dance

Your daughter's wedding

Cruise ship in international waters

Borderline OK

Your son's wedding

Dinner cruise on the Mississippi

Never OK

Clubs where you have to "know a guy" to get in

Any other clubs

YouTube

If you're thinking about buying the $75 T-shirt
with the skull-and-roses pattern, that's a good sign.
It's the people who actually buy it who are beyond hope.

To a boomer, a "thong" is thomthing you thing.

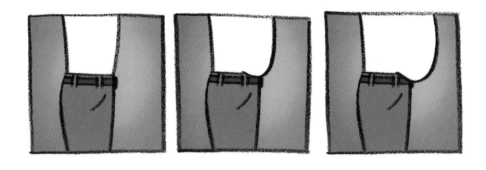

Theoretically,
ANY man can wear
the same size pants
from high school
to retirement.

How you do your hair isn't nearly as big a deal
as whether or not you have hair to do.

Bob soon realized that his hair peninsula had broken off to form its own island.

Old age is just a state . . . and that state is Florida.

If your mom had let you keep all those Barbie Dolls,
you could've sold them for enough money
to put her in a much nicer home.

You're not officially old
until you start yelling at the weatherman.

Three Things People of a Certain Age Can't Say Without Giggling

1. Twitter

2. Download

3. Nipple (no one can say that without giggling)

Cool Things About the AARP

Kind of sounds like pirate talk.

They have a really great Net site
on the Interwebs.

Did we already say,
"Kind of sounds like pirate talk"?

Simple Test to Determine if You Should Wear a Hawaiian Shirt

Look around. Are you in Hawaii?

If not, then no.

If yes, also no.

Chairs That No Longer Seem Funny

The vibrating recliner

The hook-over-the-edge-of-the-bathtub chair

The slowly-glide-up-the-stairs motorized chair

Your age is just a number.
Also, a sequoia is just a tree,
Hoover is just a dam,
and Grand is just a canyon.

The Dwarfs at 50

Squinty

Baldy

Touchy

Cranky

Drafty

Chubby

Gassy

If all the people who said they were at Woodstock
had actually been at Woodstock,
people would still be sitting in traffic
created by Woodstock.

Getting older has its perks.
You can tell anybody anything you want
about your relationship with Jimi Hendrix
and no one can prove it's not true.

As long as you can button it, zip it, snap it, or hook it, you can continue to wear it. That's the only rule.

There is probably a culture somewhere that sees nose hair as a sign of virility. But where, exactly, can we find it? The culture, not the nose hair. We KNOW where that is.

Pizza is not your friend.
It used to be, but that relationship is over.
You can break up in stages, if you must,
but you and pizza are done. (Especially sausage.)

There are several things you can do
to look and feel younger.
All the experts agree, though,
that the No. 1 thing is to be born later.

If you haven't already grown a mustache,
don't start now. Especially if you're a woman.

We had "Guitar Hero" when we were kids, too.
It was called "Pretend Mom's broom
is an electric guitar."

"Sleep number" used to seem silly.
It doesn't seem so silly now, does it?

Middle-Aged Chickens

Dignity. Wisdom. Respect. Status.

These are just four of the things we'd gladly trade
to have our eyebrows back up where they used to be.

Look at it this way: people assume you're forgetful,
so why not make it work for you?
You don't want to do something? "Forget" to do it.
Don't like somebody? "Forget" you ever met.
Remember, no one can prove what you've forgotten.

In 2025, retirement village
residents play a game of
"Guess What the Tattoo Used to Be!"

We might be the first generation to save up
our senior citizen discounts to pay for our tattoos.

Fact: Getting young men to carry stuff for you
is not only NOT embarrassing, it's actually awesome!

Selling your house and buying an RV
to travel the country seems like
a much better idea to the people who have not
sold their homes and bought an RV
to travel the country.

Remember: you're never too old to criticize the people who are younger than you. Or older. Or the same age.

It's simple. There are two kinds of music: "Sixties" and "Bad."

You're old enough to remember
singing dance songs when you couldn't dance,
surf songs when you didn't know how to surf,
and hot rod songs when you drove a
Plymouth Belvedere.

Shouldn't Cap'n Crunch be an admiral by now?

How valuably are you using the time
you used to spend combing your hair?

Suddenly, you can't get enough talk radio.

TALK RADIO FOR
PEOPLE YOUR AGE.

You know you're a boomer when you believe
the best thing about your BlackBerry
is constant access to
where the storm front currently is.

Remember when belts held something up,
rather than hold something back?

THEN: Sex in cars
NOW: Sex in RVs

No matter what the song says, do not "twist again."

As long as you've got an older sibling,
you will never truly be old.
Firstborns, you're on your own.

There's actually quite a long list of things you did
that used to embarrass your parents
that now embarrass your kids.

The good thing about wearing short skirts these days
is that from across the room, your legs
can pass for textured stockings.

NOW: iPod
THEN: iWait for the radio
to play a halfway decent song

The longer you put off using the Internet,
the more magical it seems once you finally do.

News Flash

There's a pretty good chance your mom
knew about those magazines all along.

Boomer Tip #9

As you get older, your life should be
much more in line with your goals.
Be happy if you can get all the way up a flight of stairs
or if you remembered to flip your turn signal off.

Do Not Try This at Home
(Seriously)

Do not count the number
of presidents you've lived through
and the number of sexual partners you've had
to see which number is higher.
Either way, you're sure to have disappointing results.

Having a bad memory can really work
to your advantage. For instance, you have no problem
with summer repeats of your favorite TV shows.

When 50-year-olds golf

File This Under
"What the Hell Were We Thinking?"

Clacker balls

Earth shoes

Mood rings

Cinnamon toothpicks

Troll dolls

Disco Duck

The Bay City Rollers

Now That We Know Who Deep Throat Was, Here Are Some Other Things They Should Tell Us

What did Billie Joe McAllister
throw off the Tallahatchie Bridge?

What does Charlie look like?

Where is Jimmy Hoffa?

Who was Question Mark of "? and the Mysterians"?

Who are the father, son, and holy ghost
who caught the last train for the coast?

What does Carlton the Doorman look like?
Are he and Charlie the same person?

Who did write the Book of Love?

When exactly did a cross-your-heart bra
become a cross-your-waist bra?

The trouble with getting a boob job
is that then they no longer match anything else.

Welcome to the
"Wearing a fanny pack without shame" years.

The "Missing Glasses"
Support Group

Remember how you couldn't wait for the day
when you'd never have to climb
another rope in gym class again?
That day has come.
So at least there's that.

Tommy, can you hear me?
Tommy, can you see me?
Or are you a boomer, too?

A Boomer Secret

Sometimes boomers pretend to be
talking on their cell phones
to justify their erratic driving.

Hairstyles You've Probably Had and Certainly Regret (His)

Slicked down and stood up
with enough grease to fry up some 'taters

The walking Brillo pad

The hairstyle David Cassidy would've had if he hadn't
kept a $200-an-hour stylist on retainer 24 hours a day.

The drunken barber shag

Business in the front, party in the back,
stupid pretty much everywhere

The comb-not-quite-over

Hairstyles You've Probably Had and Certainly Regret (Hers)

Forehead-stretched-like-a-trampoline pigtails

Teased until it threatened to bite you

The Dippity-Don't

The hairstyle that would've looked just like Farrah Fawcett—except you're not Farrah Fawcett

The wall of bangs that could deflect a bullet

Purple

Things It's OK to Relive

that carefree feeling of abandon

the excitement of endless possibilities for your future

dancing to the music

giving peace a chance

Things It's Not OK to Relive

going braless

More for the "What the Hell Were we Thinking?" File

Hot pants

Transactional analysis

Dr. Scholl's exercise sandals

Headbands

Go-go boots

Deely boppers

"Manimal"

White lipstick

"You're only as old as you feel"
really isn't good news most days.

THEN: Really wanted to join a movement
NOW: Just want to have a movement

Of the 400,000 people who attended Woodstock,
only about 10 million of them remember it.

One day you wake up and think, "Good! I woke up!"
And suddenly you know you're a boomer.

Boomers are caught somewhere between
"young and firm" and "old and infirm."

After a certain age, playing "doctor" becomes less sexy.

THEN: "Did it three times last night" referred to sex.

NOW: "Did it three times last night" refers to peeing.

Boomer Tip #15

If you want to stay in shape, buy a fancy
exercise machine. Or just try to stand up
out of your old beanbag chair.

How to Find the Sport That's Right for You

Step 1: Try sport.

Step 2: Evaluate. Does it hurt?

Step 3: If yes, stop. If no, stop. It'll hurt soon.

These days your favorite style of clothing is "loose."

For what growing older lacks in looks and energy,
it more than makes up for in
knowledge of the various forms of life insurance.
Not exactly a fair trade-off, though.

Being a boomer means videotaping your kid's entire life, then never watching a minute of it.

Face it. You and your kids will never agree on which was the first Star Wars.

THEN: "Good rockin'" required a dance floor.
NOW: "Good rockin'" requires a chair.

Texting is nothing but a bunch of punk kids
showing off their thumb flexibility.

Even if you had kept all that stuff
that's finally worth something on e-Bay,
you wouldn't be able to find it in the basement.

Remember when it was just "mail" without the "e"?

Being happy as you get older only takes minor adjustments to your medication.

They were both fast pill takers.
But only one could be champion.

You know you're a boomer if
you'd need a pick-up truck
if you ever wanted to carry around one thousand songs.

Remember when reality was what you
watched TV to get AWAY from?

Know what's best about an aging butt?
Aging vision.

First you believe in Santa Claus.
Then you dress up like Santa Claus.
And one day you actually look like him.
That's the one you don't see coming.

Part of the appeal of hybrid vehicles is that
anything sounds better if it has less gas.

When you hit midlife, you may want a sports car:
a small sports car that goes from zero to 60
in a relatively short time. It's understandable.
It's also a crisis. There's a reason they call it a crisis,
and not a "happy car ownership event."
Say no to the car. Avoid the crisis.

Middle-Aged Chopper
And this one has extra lumbar support, a bifocal windshield, and a built-in pill dispenser.
Cool.

You Might Be a Boomer
if You've Ever Used One of These Pick-up Lines

Your bad knee must be killing you,
because you've been walking through
my mind all evening.

Your retirement village or mine?

Do I know you from someplace? Seriously—I forget.

Can I buy you a drink with my senior discount?

If I said you had a beautiful body
would you know I was near-sighted?

Ted hoped the salt and pepper look would make him seem more distinguished.

CRAZY BIRTHDAY THEN:

Woo Hoooo!

CRAZY BIRTHDAY NOW:

I know it's after 5 o'clock, but I'm gonna order a coffee anyway.

:Gasp:

gordon.

"Over the hill" has such a negative connotation.
It's like they're saying it's
a downward slide or . . . oh. Huh.

Now that you're older, you've come to appreciate
all the things you used to take for granted,
mostly because you can't do them anymore.

Crap!

Gray hair in places you can't dye.

The so called "troubles" you had
when you were younger were really just
practice for your current, actual problems.

Theoretically, acne should make you feel young.
It's one of nature's cruel ironies that it doesn't.

Boomers will never admit to a young person
how boring life was before the Internet.

You can finally have your cake and eat it, too. Thankfully, you can also finally be seen in public wearing stretch pants.

When did an "afternoon delight" turn into a nap?

Welcome to the age of being too tired to remember when you weren't tired all the time.

Your kids tell you that you're too old
to listen to the popular music these days.
Thank God.

Now, they're only the "good butt" pants
until you put them on.

You can judge a person's age
by how far away from their house
they're willing to wear their pajamas.

A Fashion Tip
For Men Your Age:

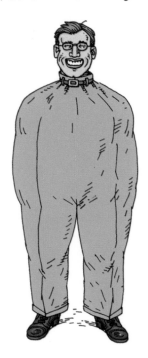

If you wear your pants
high enough, you don't
need a shirt.

Our generation were the dreamers, the radicals, the ones who could see a better world— **the visionaries!**

We may not have flying cars yet,
but we do have Viagra.
So all in all, things are working out just fine.

These days, you probably couldn't twist and NOT shout.

After all this time, life is still confusing.
Thank goodness your kids know everything.

The people who design swimsuits
ought to be tracked down and forced to look
at pictures of naked boomers.
A harsh punishment, sure, but an appropriate one.

You've reached that stage in life
where you might as well take up swing dancing.
Pretty much everything is swinging, anyway.

An apple a day might taste good and supply much-needed fiber, but at your age, there's no way it'll keep the doctor away.

50 is the new 30, except totally worse.

Any day now, you're going to decide what you want to be when you grow up.

When old guys dream.

If you have enjoyed this book,
we would love to hear from you.
(So please speak VERY loud.)

Please send your comments to:

Hallmark Book Feedback
P.O. Box 419034
Mail Drop 215
Kansas City, MO 64141

Or e-mail us at:

booknotes@hallmark.com